THE
HARLEM
GHETTO

THE
HARLEM
GHETTO

Essays

JAMES BALDWIN

BEACON PRESS
BOSTON

BEACON PRESS
Boston, Massachusetts
www.beacon.org

Beacon Press books
are published under the auspices of
the Unitarian Universalist Association of Congregations.

This book is printed on acid-free paper that meets
the uncoated paper ANSI/NISO specifications for
permanence as revised in 1992.

Author photo by Carl Van Vechten, printed with permission
of the Van Vechten Trust and acquired from the Beinecke
Rare Book and Manuscript Library, Yale University.

Text design and composition by Kim Arney

Library of Congress Cataloging-in-Publication
Data is available for this title.
ISBN: 978-0-8070-1865-1; e-book: 978-0-8070-1866-8

CONTENTS

THE
HARLEM
GHETTO

THE HARLEM GHETTO

H ARLEM, PHYSICALLY AT LEAST, has changed very little in my parents' lifetime or in mine. Now as then the buildings are old and in desperate need of repair, the streets are crowded and dirty, there are too many human beings per square block. Rents are 10 to 58 per cent higher than anywhere else in the city; food, expensive everywhere, is more expensive here and of an inferior quality; and now that the war is over and money is dwindling, clothes are carefully shopped for and seldom bought. Negroes, traditionally the last to be hired and the first to be fired, are finding jobs harder to get, and, while prices are rising implacably, wages are going down. All over Harlem now there is felt the same bitter expectancy with which, in my childhood, we awaited winter: it is coming and it will be hard; there is nothing anyone can do about it.

All of Harlem is pervaded by a sense of congestion, rather like the insistent, maddening, claustrophobic pounding in the skull that comes from trying to breathe in a very small room with all the windows shut. Yet the white man walking through Harlem is not at all likely to find it sinister or more wretched than any other slum.

Harlem wears to the casual observer a casual face; no one remarks that—considering the history of black men and women and the legends that have sprung up about them, to say nothing of the ever-present policemen, wary on the street corners—the face is, indeed, somewhat excessively casual and may not be as open or as careless as it seems. If an outbreak of more than usual violence occurs, as in 1935 or in 1943, it is met with sorrow and surprise and rage; the social hostility of the rest of the city feeds on this as proof that they were right all along, and the hostility increases; speeches are made, committees are set up, investigations ensue. Steps are taken to right the wrong, without, however, expanding or demolishing the ghetto. The idea is to make it less of a social liability, a process about as helpful as make-up to a leper. Thus, we have the Boys' Club on West 134th Street, the playground at West 131st and Fifth Avenue; and, since Negroes will not be allowed to live in Stuyvesant Town, Metropolitan Life is thoughtfully erecting a housing project called Riverton in the center of Harlem; however, it is not likely that any but the professional class of Negroes—and not all of them—will be able to pay the rent.

Most of these projects have been stimulated by perpetually embattled Negro leaders and by the Negro press. Concerning Negro leaders, the best that one can say is that they are in an impossible position and that the handful motivated by genuine concern maintain this position with heartbreaking dignity. It is unlikely that anyone acquainted with Harlem seriously assumes that the presence of one playground more or less has any profound effect upon the psychology of the citizens there. And yet it is better to have the playground; it is better than nothing; and it will, at least, make life somewhat easier for parents who will then know that their children are not in as much danger of being run down in the streets. Similarly, even though the American cult of literacy has chiefly operated only to provide a market for the *Reader's Digest* and the *Daily News*, literacy is still better than illiteracy; so Negro leaders must demand more and better schools for Negroes, though any Negro who takes this schooling at face value will find himself virtually incapacitated for life in this democracy. Possibly the most salutary effect of all this activity is that it assures the Negro that he is not altogether forgotten: people *are* working in his behalf, however hopeless or misguided they may be; and as long as the water is troubled it cannot become stagnant.

The terrible thing about being a Negro leader lies in the term itself. I do not mean merely the somewhat condescending differentiation the term implies, but the nicely refined torture a man can experience from having been created and defeated by the same circumstances. That is, Negro leaders have been created by the American scene, which thereafter works against them at every point; and the best that they can hope for is ultimately to work themselves out of their jobs, to nag contemporary

American leaders and the members of their own group until a bad situation becomes so complicated and so bad that it cannot be endured any longer. It is like needling a blister until it bursts. On the other hand, one cannot help observing that some Negro leaders and politicians are far more concerned with their careers than with the welfare of Negroes, and their dramatic and publicized battles are battles with the wind. Again, this phenomenon cannot be changed without a change in the American scene. In a land where, it is said, any citizen can grow up and become president, Negroes can be pardoned for desiring to enter Congress.

The Negro press, which supports any man, provided he is sufficiently dark and well-known—with the exception of certain Negro novelists accused of drawing portraits unflattering to the race—has for years received vastly confusing criticism based on the fact that it is helplessly and always exactly what it calls itself, that is, a press devoted entirely to happenings in or about the Negro world. This preoccupation can probably be forgiven in view of the great indifference and frequent hostility of the American white press. The Negro press has been accused of not helping matters much—as indeed, it has not, nor do I see how it could have. And it has been accused of being sensational, which it is; but this is a criticism difficult to take seriously in a country so devoted to the sensational as ours.

The best-selling Negro newspaper, I believe, is the *Amsterdam Star-News*, which is also the worst, being gleefully devoted to murders, rapes, raids on love-nests, interracial wars, any item—however meaningless—concerning prominent Negroes, and whatever racial gains can be reported for the week—all in just about that order. Apparently, this policy works well; it sells papers—which is, after all, the aim; in my childhood we never missed an edition. The day the paper came out we could hear, far down the street, the news vendor screaming the latest scandal and people rushing to read about it.

The *Amsterdam* has been rivaled, in recent years, by the *People's Voice*, a journal, modeled on *PM* and referred to as *PV*. *PV* is not so wildly sensational a paper as the *Amsterdam*, though its coverage is much the same (the news coverage of the Negro press is naturally pretty limited). *PV*'s politics are less murky, to the left of center (the *Amsterdam* is Republican, a political affiliation that has led it into some strange doubletalk), and its tone, since its inception, has been ever more hopelessly militant, full of warnings, appeals, and open letters to the government—which, to no one's surprise, are not answered—and the same rather pathetic

preoccupation with prominent Negroes and what
they are doing. Columns signed by Lena Horne and
Paul Robeson appeared in *PV* until several weeks
ago, when both severed their connections with the
paper. Miss Horne's column made her sound like
an embittered Eleanor Roosevelt, and the only column of Robeson's I have read was concerned with
the current witch-hunt in Hollywood, discussing
the kind of movies under attack and Hollywood's
traditional treatment of Negroes. It is personally
painful to me to realize that so gifted and forceful
a man as Robeson should have been tricked by
his own bitterness and by a total inability to understand the nature of political power in general,
or Communist aims in particular, into missing
the point of his own critique, which is worth a
great deal of thought: that there are a great many
ways of being un-American, some of them nearly
as old as the country itself, and that the House

Un-American Activities Committee might find concepts and attitudes even more damaging to American life in a picture like *Gone With the Wind* than in the possibly equally romantic but far less successful *Watch on the Rhine*.

The only other newspapers in the field with any significant sale in Harlem are the Pittsburgh *Courier*, which has the reputation of being the best of the lot, and the *Afro-American*, which resembles the New York *Journal-American* in layout and type and seems to make a consistent if unsuccessful effort to be at once readable, intelligent, and fiery. The *Courier* is a high-class paper, reaching its peak in the handling of its society news and in the columns of George S. Schuyler, whose Olympian serenity infuriates me, but who, as a matter of fact, reflects with great accuracy the state of mind and the ambitions of the professional, well-to-do Negro who has managed to find a place to stand.

Mr. Schuyler, who is remembered still for a satirical novel I have not read, called *Black No More*, is aided enormously in this position by a genteel white wife and a child-prodigy daughter—who is seriously regarded in some circles as proof of the incomprehensible contention that the mating of white and black is more likely to produce genius than any other combination. (The *Afro-American* recently ran a series of articles on this subject, "The Education of a Genius," by Mrs. Amarintha Work, who recorded in detail the development of her mulatto son, Craig.)

Ebony and *Our World* are the two big magazines in the field, *Ebony* looking and sounding very much like *Life*, and *Our World* being the black man's *Look*. *Our World* is a very strange, disorganized magazine indeed, sounding sometimes like a college newspaper and sometimes like a call to arms, but principally, like its more skillful brothers, devoted to the proposition that anything a white man can do a Negro can probably do better. *Ebony* digs feature articles out of such things as the "real" Lena Horne and Negro FBI agents, and it travels into the far corners of the earth for any news, however trivial, concerning any Negro or group of Negroes who are in any way unusual and/or newsworthy. The tone of both *Ebony* and *Our World* is affirmative; they cater to the "better class of Negro." *Ebony's* November 1947 issue carried an editoral entitled "Time To Count Our Blessings," which began by accusing Chester Himes (author of the novel *Lonely Crusade*) of having a color psychosis, and went on to explain that there are Negro racists also who are just as blind and dangerous as Bilbo, which is incontestably true, and that, compared to the millions of starving Europeans, Negroes are sitting pretty—which comparison, I hazard, cannot possibly mean anything to any Negro who has not seen

Europe. The editorial concluded that Negroes had come a long way and that "as patriotic Americans" it was time "we" stopped singing the blues and realized just how bright the future was. These cheering sentiments were flanked—or underscored, if you will—by a photograph on the opposite page of an aging Negro farm woman carrying home a bumper crop of onions. It apparently escaped the editors of *Ebony* that the very existence of their magazine, and its table of contents for any month, gave the lie to this effort to make the best of a bad bargain.

The true *raison d'être* of the Negro press can be found in the letters-to-the-editor sections, where the truth about life among the rejected can be seen in print. It is the terrible dilemma of the Negro press that, having no other model, it models itself on the white press, attempting to emulate the same effortless, sophisticated tone—a tone its subject matter renders utterly unconvincing. It is simply impossible not to sing the blues, audibly or not, when the lives lived by Negroes are so inescapably harsh and stunted. It is not the Negro press that is at fault: whatever contradictions, inanities, and political infantilism can be charged to it can be charged equally to the American press at large. It is a black man's newspaper straining for recognition and a foothold in the white man's world. Matters are not helped in the least by the fact that the white man's world, intellectually, morally, and spiritually, has the meaningless ring of a hollow drum and the odor of slow death. Within the body of the Negro press all the wars and falsehoods, all the decay and dislocation and struggle of our society are seen in relief.

The Negro press, like the Negro, becomes the scapegoat for our ills. There is no difference, after all, between the *Amsterdam*'s handling of a murder on Lenox Avenue and the *Daily News'* coverage of

a murder on Beekman Hill; nor is there any difference between the chauvinism of the two papers,
except that the *News* is smug and the *Amsterdam* is
desperate. Negroes live violent lives, unavoidably;
a Negro press without violence is therefore not
possible; and, further, in every act of violence, particularly violence against white men, Negroes feel a
certain thrill of identification, a wish to have done
it themselves, a feeling that old scores are being
settled at last. It is no accident that Joe Louis is the
most idolized man in Harlem. He has succeeded on
a level that white America indicates is the only level
for which it has any respect. We (Americans in general, that is) like to point to Negroes and to most
of their activities with a kind of tolerant scorn; but
it is ourselves we are watching, ourselves we are
damning, or—condescendingly—bending to save.

I have written at perhaps excessive length
about the Negro press, principally because its

many critics have always seemed to me to make the irrational demand that the nation's most oppressed minority behave itself at all times with a skill and foresight no one ever expected of the late Joseph Patterson or ever expected of Hearst; and I have tried to give some idea of its tone because it seems to me that it is here that the innate desperation is betrayed. As for the question of Negro advertising, which has caused so much comment, it seems to me quite logical that any minority identified by the color of its skin and the texture of its hair would eventually grow self-conscious about these attributes and avoid advertising lotions that made the hair kinkier and soaps that darkened the skin. The American ideal, after all, is that everyone should be as much alike as possible.

It is axiomatic that the Negro is religious, which is to say that he stands in fear of the God our ancestors gave us and before whom we all tremble yet. There are probably more churches in Harlem than in any other ghetto in this city and they are going full blast every night and some of them are filled with praying people every day. This, supposedly, exemplifies the Negro's essential simplicity and good-will; but it is actually a fairly desperate emotional business.

These churches range from the august and publicized Abyssinian Baptist Church on West 138th Street to resolutely unclassifiable lofts, basements, store-fronts, and even private dwellings. Nightly, Holyroller ministers, spiritualists, self-appointed prophets and Messiahs gather their flocks together for worship and for strength through joy. And this is not, as *Cabin in the Sky* would have us believe, merely a childlike emotional release. Their faith may be described as childlike, but the end it serves is often sinister. It may, indeed, "keep them happy"—a phrase carrying the inescapable inference that the way of life imposed on Negroes makes them quite actively unhappy—but also, and much more significantly, religion operates here as a complete and exquisite fantasy revenge: white people own the earth and commit all manner of abomination and injustice on it; the bad will be punished and the good rewarded, for God is not sleeping, the judgment is not far off. It does not require a spectacular degree of perception to realize that bitterness is here neither dead nor sleeping, and that the white man, believing what he wishes to believe, has misread the symbols. Quite often the Negro preacher descends to levels less abstract and leaves no doubt as to what is on his mind: the pressure of life in Harlem, the conduct of the Italian-Ethiopian war, racial injustice during the recent war, and the terrible possibility of yet another very soon. All these topics provide excellent springboards for sermons thinly coated with spirituality but designed mainly to illustrate the injustice of the white American and anticipate his certain and long overdue punishment.

Here, too, can be seen one aspect of the Negro's ambivalent relation to the Jew. To begin with, though the traditional Christian accusation that the Jews killed Christ is neither questioned nor doubted, the term "Jew" actually operates in this initial context to include all infidels of white skin who have failed to accept the Savior. No real distinction is made: the preacher begins by accusing the Jews of having refused the light and proceeds from there to a catalog of their subsequent sins and the sufferings visited on them by a wrathful God. Though the notion of the suffering is based on the image of the wandering, exiled Jew, the context changes imperceptibly, to become a fairly obvious reminder of the trials of the Negro, while the sins recounted are the sins of the American republic.

At this point, the Negro identifies himself almost wholly with the Jew. The more devout Negro considers that he *is* a Jew, in bondage to a hard taskmaster and waiting for a Moses to lead him out of Egypt. The hymns, the texts, and the most favored legends of the devout Negro are all Old Testament and therefore Jewish in origin: the flight from Egypt, the Hebrew children in the fiery furnace, the terrible jubilee songs of deliverance: *Lord, wasn't that hard trials, great tribulations, I'm bound to leave this land!* The covenant God made in the beginning with Abraham and which was to extend to his children and to his children's children forever is a covenant made with these latter-day exiles also: as Israel was chosen, so are they. The birth and death of Jesus, which adds a non-Judaic element, also implements this identification. It is the covenant made with Abraham again, renewed, signed with his blood. ("Before

Abraham was, I am.") Here the figure of Jesus operates as the intercessor, the bridge from earth to heaven; it was Jesus who made it possible, who made salvation free to all, "to the Jew first and afterwards the Gentile." The images of the suffering Christ and the suffering Jew are wedded with the image of the suffering slave, and they are one: the people that walked in darkness have seen a great light.

But if the Negro has bought his salvation with pain and the New Testament is used to prove, as it were, the validity of the transformation, it is the Old Testament which is clung to and most frequently preached from, which provides the emotional fire and anatomizes the path of bondage; and which promises vengeance and assures the chosen of their place in Zion. The favorite text of my father, among the most earnest of ministers, was not "Father, forgive them, for they know not what they do," but "How can I sing the Lord's song in a strange land?"

This same identification, which Negroes, since slavery, have accepted with their mothers' milk, serves, in contemporary actuality, to implement an involved and specific bitterness. Jews in Harlem are small tradesmen, rent collectors, real estate agents, and pawnbrokers; they operate in accordance with the American business tradition of exploiting Negroes, and they are therefore identified with oppression and are hated for it. I remember meeting no Negro in the years of my growing up, in my family or out of it, who would really ever trust a Jew, and few who did not, indeed, exhibit for them the blackest contempt. On the other hand, this did not prevent their working for Jews, being utterly civil and pleasant to them, and, in most cases, contriving to delude their employers into believing that, far from harboring any dislike for Jews, they would rather work for a Jew than for anyone else. It is part of the price the Negro pays for his position in this society that, as Richard Wright points out, he is almost always acting. A Negro learns to gauge precisely what reaction the alien person facing him desires, and he produces it with disarming artlessness. The friends I had, growing up and going to work, grew more bitter every day; and, conversely, they learned to hide this bitterness and to fit into the pattern Gentile and Jew alike had fixed for them.

The tension between Negroes and Jews contains an element not characteristic of Negro-Gentile tension, an element which accounts in some measure for the Negro's tendency to castigate the Jew verbally more often than the Gentile, and which might lead one to the conclusion that, of all white people on the face of the earth, it is the Jew whom the Negro hates most.

When the Negro hates the Jew *as a Jew* he does so partly because the nation does and in much the same painful fashion that he hates himself. It is an aspect of his humiliation whittled down to a manageable size and then transferred; it is the best form the Negro has for tabulating vocally his long record of grievances against his native land.

At the same time, there is a subterranean assumption that the Jew should "know better," that he has suffered enough himself to know what suffering means. An understanding is expected of the Jew such as none but the most naïve and visionary Negro has ever expected of the American Gentile. The Jew, by the nature of his own precarious position, has failed to vindicate this faith. Jews, like Negroes, must use every possible weapon in order to be accepted, and must try to cover their vulnerability by a frenzied adoption of the customs of the country; and the nation's treatment of Negroes is unquestionably a custom. The Jew has been taught—and, too often, accepts—the legend of Negro inferiority; and the Negro, on the other hand, has found nothing in his experience with Jews to counteract the legend of Semitic greed. Here the American white Gentile has two legends serving him at once: he has divided these minorities and he rules.

It seems unlikely that within this complicated structure any real and systematic cooperation can be achieved between Negroes and Jews. (This is in terms of the over-all social problem and is not meant to imply that individual friendships are impossible or that they are valueless when they occur.) The structure of the American commonwealth has trapped both these minorities into attitudes of perpetual hostility. They do not dare trust each other—the Jew because he feels he must climb higher on the American social ladder and has, so far as he is concerned, nothing to gain from identification with any minority even more unloved than he; while the Negro is in the even less tenable position of not really daring to trust anyone.

This applies, with qualifications and yet with almost no exceptions, even to those Negroes called progressive and "unusual." Negroes of the professional class (as distinct from professional Negroes) compete actively with the Jew in daily contact; and they wear anti-Semitism as a defiant proof of their citizenship; their positions are too shaky to allow them any real ease or any faith in anyone. They do not trust whites or each other or themselves; and, particularly and vocally, they do not trust Jews. During my brief days as a Socialist I spent more than one meeting arguing against anti-Semitism with a Negro college student, who was trying to get into civil service and was supporting herself

THE HARLEM GHETTO ▪ 27

meanwhile as a domestic. She was by no means a stupid girl, nor even a particularly narrow-minded one: she was all in favor of the millennium, even to working with Jews to achieve it; but she was not prepared ever to accept a Jew as a friend. It did no good to point out, as I did, that the exploitation of which she accused the Jews was American, not Jewish, that in fact, behind the Jewish face stood the American reality. And *my* Jewish friends in high school were not like that, I said, they had no intention of exploiting *me*, we did not hate each other. (I remember, as I spoke, being aware of doubt crawling like fog in the back of my mind.) This might all be very well, she told me, we were children now, with no need to earn a living. Wait until later, when your friends go into business and you try to get a job. You'll see!

It is this bitterness—felt alike by the inarticu-late, hungry population of Harlem, by the wealthy

on Sugar Hill, and by the brilliant exceptions en-
sconced in universities——which has defeated and
promises to continue to defeat all efforts at interracial understanding. I am not one of the people
who believe that oppression imbues a people with
wisdom or insight or sweet charity, though the
survival of the Negro in this country would simply not have been possible if this bitterness had
been all he felt. In America, though, life seems to
move faster than anywhere else on the globe and
each generation is promised more than it will get:
which creates, in each generation, a furious, bewildered rage, the rage of people who cannot find
solid ground beneath their feet. Just as a mountain
of sociological investigations, committee reports,
and plans for recreational centers have failed to
change the face of Harlem or prevent Negro boys
and girls from growing up and facing, individually
and alone, the unendurable frustration of being

always, everywhere, inferior—until finally the cancer attacks the mind and warps it—so there seems no hope for better Negro-Jewish relations without a change in the American pattern.

Both the Negro and the Jew are helpless; the pressure of living is too immediate and incessant to allow time for understanding. I can conceive of no Negro native to this country who has not, by the age of puberty, been irreparably scarred by the conditions of his life. All over Harlem, Negro boys and girls are growing into stunted maturity, trying desperately to find a place to stand; and the wonder is not that so many are ruined but that so many survive. The Negro's outlets are desperately constricted. In his dilemma he turns first upon himself and then upon whatever most represents to him his own emasculation. Here the Jew is caught in the American crossfire. The Negro, facing a Jew, hates, at bottom, not his Jewishness but the color of his skin. It is not the Jewish tradition by which he has been betrayed but the tradition of his native land. But just as a society must have a scapegoat, so hatred must have a symbol. Georgia has the Negro and Harlem has the Jew.

JOURNEY TO ATLANTA

THE PROGRESSIVE PARTY HAS NOT, so far as I can gather, made any very great impression in Harlem, and this is not so much despite as because of its campaign promises, promises rather too extravagant to be believed. It is considered a rather cheerful axiom that all Americans distrust politicians. (No one takes the further and less cheerful step of considering just what effect this mutual contempt has on either the public or the politicians, who have, indeed, very little to do with one another.) Of all Americans, Negroes distrust politicians most, or, more accurately, they have been best trained to expect nothing from them; more than other Americans, they are always aware of the enormous gap between election promises and their daily lives. It is true that the promises excite them, but this is not because they are taken as proof of good intentions. They are the proof of something more concrete than intentions: that the Negro situation is not static, that changes have occurred, and are occurring and will occur—this, in spite of the daily, dead-end monotony. It is this daily, dead-end monotony, though, as well as the wise desire not to be betrayed by too much hoping, which causes them to look on politicians with such an extraordinarily disenchanted eye.

This fatalistic indifference is something that drives the optimistic American liberal quite mad; he is prone, in his more exasperated moments, to refer to Negroes as political children,

THE HARLEM GHETTO   **33**

an appellation not entirely just. Negro liberals, being consulted, assure us that this is something that will disappear with "education," a vast, all-purpose term, conjuring up visions of sunlit housing projects, stacks of copybooks and a race of well-soaped, dark-skinned people who never slur their R's. Actually, this is not so much political irresponsibility as the product of experience, experience which no amount of education can quite efface. It is, as much as anything else, the reason the Negro vote is so easily bought and sold, the reason for that exclamation heard so frequently on Sugar Hill: "Our people never get anywhere."

"Our people" have functioned in this country for nearly a century as political weapons, the trump card up the enemies' sleeve; anything promised Negroes at election time is also a threat levelled at the opposition; in the struggle for mastery the Negro is the pawn. It is inescapable that this is only possible because of his position in this country and it has very frequently seemed at least equally apparent that this is a position which no one, least of all the politician, seriously intended to change.

Since Negroes have been in this country their one major, devastating gain was their Emancipation, an emancipation no one regards any more as having been dictated by humanitarian impulses. All that has followed from that brings to mind the rather unfortunate image of bones thrown to a pack of dogs sufficiently hungry to be dangerous. If all this sounds rather deliberately grim, it is not through any wish to make the picture darker than it is; I would merely like to complete the picture usually presented by pointing out that no matter how many instances there have been of genuine concern and good-will, nor how many hard, honest struggles have been carried on to improve the position of the Negro people, their position has not, in fact, changed so far as most of them are concerned.

Sociologists and historians, having the historical perspective in mind, may conclude that we are moving toward ever-greater democracy; but this is beyond the ken of a Negro growing up in any one of this country's ghettos. As regards Negro politicians, they are considered with pride as *politicians*, a pride much akin to that felt concerning Marian Anderson or Joe Louis: they have proven the worth of the Negro people and in terms, American terms, which no one can negate. But as no housewife expects Marian Anderson's genius to be of any practical aid in her dealings with the landlord, so nothing is expected of Negro representatives. The terrible thing, and here we have an American phenomenon in relief, is the fact that the Negro representative, by virtue of his position, is ever more removed from the people he ostensibly serves. Moreover, irrespective of personal integrity, his position—neatly and often painfully paradoxical—is utterly dependent on the continuing debasement of fourteen million Negroes; should the national ideals be put into practice tomorrow, countless prominent Negroes would lose their *raison d'être*.

Finally, we are confronted with the psychology and tradition of the country; if the Negro vote is so easily bought and sold, it is because it has been treated with so little respect; since no Negro dares seriously assume that any politician is concerned with the fate of Negroes, or would do much about it if he had the power, the vote must be bartered for what it will get, for whatever short-term goals can be managed. These goals are mainly economic and frequently personal, sometimes pathetic: bread or a new roof or five dollars, or, continuing up the

scale, schools, houses or more Negroes in hith-
erto Caucasian jobs. The American commonwealth
chooses to overlook what Negroes are never able
to forget: they are not *really* considered a part of
it. Like Aziz in *A Passage to India* or Topsy in *Uncle
Tom's Cabin*, they know that white people, whatever
their love for justice, have no love for them.

This is the crux of the matter; and the Progressive Party, with its extravagant claims, has, therefore, imposed on itself the considerable burden
of proof. The only party within recent memory
which made equally strident claims of fellowship
were the Communists, who failed to survive this
test; and the only politician of similar claims was,
of course, Wallace's erstwhile master, Roosevelt,
who did not after all, now that the magic of his
voice is gone, succeed in raising the darker brother
to the status of a citizen. This is the ancestry of the
Wallace party, and it does not work wholly in its

favor. It operates to give pause to even the most desperate and the most gullible.

It is, however, considered on one level, the level of short-term goals, with approval, since it does afford temporary work for Negroes, particularly those associated in any manner with the arts. The rather flippant question on 125th Street now is: "So? You working for Mr. Wallace these days?" For at least there is that: entertainers, personalities are in demand. To forestall lawsuits, I must explain that I am not discussing "names"—who are in rather a different position, too touchy and complex to analyze here—but the unknown, the struggling, endless armies of Negro boys and girls bent on, and as yet very far from, recognition. A segment of this army, a quartet called *The Melodeers*, made a trip to Atlanta under the auspices of the Progressive Party in August, a trip which lasted about eighteen days and which left them with no love for Mr. Wallace. Since this quartet included two of my brothers, I was given the details of the trip; indeed, David, the younger, kept a sort of journal for me—literally a blow-by-blow account.

Harlem is filled with churches and on Sundays it gives the impression of being filled with music. Quartets such as my brothers' travel from church to church in the fashion of circuit preachers, singing as much for the love of singing and the need for practice as for the rather indifferent sums collected for them which are then divided. These quartets have "battles of song," the winning team adding, of course, immensely to its prestige, the most consistent winners being the giants in this field. The aim of all these quartets, of course, is to branch out, to hit the big time and sing for a livelihood. The Golden Gate Quartet, judging at least from its music, had its roots here, and out of such a background came Sister Rosetta Tharpe, whom I heard, not quite ten years ago, plunking a guitar in a storefront church on Fifth Avenue. *The Melodeers* have not been singing very long and are very far from well-known, and the invitation to sing on tour with the Wallace party in the South seemed, whatever their misgivings about the Mason-Dixon line, too good an opportunity to pass up.

This invitation, by the way, seems to have been the brainstorm of a Clarence Warde, a Negro merchant seaman once employed as a cottage father in a corrective institution up-state; it was he in New York who acted as a go-between, arranging, since *The Melodeers* are minors, to be their legal guardian and manager on the road. An extended tour, such as was planned, met with some opposition from the parents, an opposition countered by the possible long-term benefits of the tour in so far as the boys' careers were concerned and, even more urgently, by the assurance that, at the very least, the boys would come home with a considerably larger sum of money than any of them were making on their jobs. (The political implications do not seem to have carried much weight.) A series of churches had been lined up for them presumably throughout the South. "The understanding," writes David, "was that we were supposed to sing"; after which the party was to take over to make speeches and circulate petitions. "The arrangement," David notes laconically, "sounded very promising, so we decided to go."

And, indeed, they traveled South in splendor, in a Pullman, to be exact, in which, since what David describes as a "Southern gentleman and wife" took exception to their presence, they traveled alone.

At the Wallace headquarters in Atlanta they were introduced to a Mrs. Branson Price, a grey-haired white woman of incurably aristocratic leanings who seems to have been the directress of the party in that region. The graciousness of her reception was only slightly marred by the fact that she was not expecting singers and thought they were a new group of canvassers. She arranged for them to take rooms on Butler Street at the YMCA. Here the first gap between promise and performance was made manifest, a gap, they felt, which was perhaps too trifling to make a fuss about. In New York they had been promised comparative privacy, two to a room; but now, it developed, they were to sleep in a dormitory. This gap, in fact, it was the province of Mr. Warde to close, but whether he was simply weary from the trip or overwhelmed by the aristocratic Mrs. Price, he kept his mouth shut and, indeed, did not open it again for quite some time.

When they returned to headquarters, somewhat irritated at having had to wait three hours for the arrival of Louis Burner, who had the money for their rooms, Mrs. Price suggested that they go out canvassing. This was wholly unexpected, since no one had mentioned canvassing in New York and, since, moreover, canvassers are voluntary workers who are not paid. Further, the oldest of them was twenty, which was not voting age, and none of them knew anything about the Progressive Party, nor did they care much. On the other hand, it is somewhat difficult to refuse a grey-haired, aristocratic lady who is toiling day and night for the benefit of your people; and Mr. Warde, who should have been their spokesman, had not yet recovered his voice; so they took the petitions, which were meant to put the Wallace party on the ballot, and began knocking on doors in the Negro section of Atlanta. They were sent out in pairs, white and black, a political device which operates not only as the living proof of brotherhood, but which has the additional virtue of intimidating into passive silence the more susceptible beholder, who cannot, after all, unleash the impatient scorn he may feel with a strange, benevolent white man sitting in his parlor.

They canvassed for three days, during which time their expenses—$2.25 per man per day—were paid, but during which time they were doing no singing and making no money. On the third day they pointed out that this was not quite what they had been promised in New York, to be met with another suggestion from the invincible Mrs. Price: how would they like to sing on the sound-truck? They had not the faintest desire to sing on a sound-truck, especially when they had been promised a string of churches; however, the churches, along with Mr. Warde's vigor, seemed unavailable at the moment; they could hardly sit around Atlanta doing nothing; and so long as they worked with the party they were certain, at least, to be fed. "The purpose of our singing," David writes, "was to draw a crowd so the party could make speeches." Near the end of the singing and during the speeches, leaflets and petitions were circulated through the crowd.

David had not found Negroes in the South different in any important respect from Negroes in the North; except that many of them were distrustful and "they are always talking about the North; they have to let you know they know somebody in New York or Chicago or Detroit." Of the crowds that gathered—and, apparently, *The Melodeers* attracted great numbers—"many of these people couldn't read or write their names" and not many of them knew anything at all about the Progressive Party. But they did divine, as American Negroes must, what was expected of them; and they listened to the speeches and signed the petitions.

Becoming both desperate and impatient, *The Melodeers* began making engagements and singing on their own, stealing time from canvassing to rehearse. They made more appointments than they were able to keep; partly because the lack of money limited their mobility but also because the Party, discovering these clandestine appointments, moved in, demanding to be heard. Those churches which refused to make room for the Party were not allowed to hear the quartet, which thus lost its last hope of making any money. The quartet wondered what had happened to Mr. Warde. David's account all but ignores him until nearly the end of the trip, when his position during all this is perhaps given some illumination.

Things now began to go steadily worse. They got into an argument with the manager of the Y, who objected to their rehearsing, and moved to a private home, for which the Party paid 75¢ per man per day; and the Party, which was, one gathers, furiously retrenching, arranged for them to eat at Fraziers' Cafe, a Negro establishment on Hunter Street, for $1.25 per man per day. My correspondent notes that they had no choice of meals—"they served us what they liked"—which seems to have been mainly limp vegetables—and "we were as hungry when we walked out as we were when we walked in." On the other hand, they were allowed to choose their beverage: tea or coffee or soda pop.

Heaven only knows what prompted Mrs. Branson Price to give a party at this point. Perhaps the campaign was going extraordinarily well; perhaps Fraziers' Cafe, where the party was held, was in need of a little extra revenue as well as the knowledge that its adoption of the Party would help to bring about a better world; perhaps Mrs.

Price merely longed to be a gracious hostess once
again. In any case, on a Sunday night she gave a
party to which everyone was invited. My brother,
who at this point was much concerned with food,
observed glumly, "We had ice-cream."

The quartet sat at a table by itself, robbed,
however, of the presence of Mr. Warde, who was
invited to sit at Mrs. Price's table: "she said it
would be an honor," my correspondent notes, fail-
ing, however, to say for whom. "There was a man
there called a *folk*-singer," says David with venom,
"and, naturally, everybody had to hear some *folk*
songs." Eventually, the folksy aspect of the evening
was exhausted and the quartet was invited to sing.
They sang four selections, apparently to everyone's
delight for they had to be quite adamant about not
singing a fifth. The strain of continual singing in
the open air had done their voices no good and it
had made one of them extremely hoarse. So they

refused, over loud protests, and apologized. "This displeased Mrs. Price."

Indeed, it had. She was not in the least accustomed to having her suggestions, to say nothing of her requests, refused. Early Monday morning she called Mr. Warde to her office to inquire who those black boys thought they were? and determined to ship them all back that same day in a car. Mr. Warde, who, considering the honors of the evening before, must have been rather astounded, protested such treatment, to be warned that she might very well ship them off without a car; the six of them might very well be forced to take to the road. This is not a pleasant mode of traveling for a Negro in the North and no Negro in Atlanta, particularly no Northern Negro, is likely to get very far. Mr. Warde temporized: they could not leave on such short notice; for one thing, the boys had clothes at the cleaners which would not be ready for a while and which they could hardly afford to lose. Mrs. Price, every aristocratic vein pounding, did not wish to be concerned with such plebeian matters and, finally, losing all patience, commanded Mr. Warde to leave her office: Had he forgotten that he was in Georgia? Didn't he know better than sit in a white woman's office?

Mr. Warde, in whose bowels last night's bread of fellowship must have acquired the weight of rock, left the office. Then the quartet attempted to secure an audience; to be met with implacable refusal and the threat of the police. There were, incidentally, according to my brother, five Negro policemen in Atlanta at this time, who, though they were not allowed to arrest whites, would, of course, be willing, indeed, in their position, anxious, to arrest any Negro who seemed to need it. In Harlem, Negro policemen are feared even more than whites, for they have more to prove and fewer ways to prove it. The prospect of being arrested in Atlanta made them a little dizzy with terror: what might mean a beating in Harlem might quite possibly mean death here. "And at the same time," David says, "it was funny"; by which he means that the five policemen were faint prophecies of that equality which is the Progressive Party's goal.

They did not see Mrs. Price again; this was their severance from the Party, which now refused to pay any expenses; it was only the fact that their rent had been paid in advance which kept them off the streets. Food, however, remained a problem. Mr. Warde brought them a "couple of loaves of bread" and some jam; they sang one engagement. During this week Mrs. Price relented enough to get their clothes from the cleaners and send Mr. Warde, in custody of a white man who had been at the party, to the bus station for tickets. This man, whose resemblance to the Southern Gentleman of the Pullman is in no way diminished by his allegiance to Mr. Wallace, bought the tickets and threw them on the ground at Mr. Warde's feet, advising him not to show his black face in Georgia again.

The quartet, meanwhile, had gotten together six dollars doing odd jobs, which was enough, perhaps, for three of them to eat on the road. They split up, three leaving that Friday and the other two staying on about ten days longer, working for a construction company. Mr. Warde stopped off to visit his family, promising to see *The Melodeers* in New York, but he had not arrived as this was being written. *The Melodeers* laugh about their trip now, that good-natured, hearty laughter which is, according to white men, the peculiar heritage of Negroes, Negroes who were born with the fortunate ability to laugh all their troubles away. Somewhat surprisingly, they are not particularly bitter toward the Progressive Party, though they can scarcely be numbered among its supporters. "They're all the same," David tells me, "ain't none of 'em gonna do you no good; if you gonna be foolish enough to believe what they say, then it serves you good and right. Ain't none of 'em gonna do a thing for *me*."

NOTES OF A
NATIVE SON

ON THE 29TH OF JULY, in 1943, my father died. On the same day, a few hours later, his last child was born. Over a month before this, while all our energies were concentrated in waiting for these events, there had been, in Detroit, one of the bloodiest race riots of the century. A few hours after my father's funeral, while he lay in state in the undertaker's chapel, a race riot broke out in Harlem. On the morning of the 3rd of August, we drove my father to the graveyard through a wilderness of smashed plate glass.

The day of my father's funeral had also been my nineteenth birthday. As we drove him to the graveyard, the spoils of injustice, anarchy, discontent, and hatred were all around us. It seemed to me that God himself had devised, to mark my father's end, the most sustained and brutally dissonant of codas. And it seemed to me, too, that the violence which rose all about us as my father left the world had been devised as a corrective for the pride of his eldest son. I had declined to believe in that apocalypse which had been central to my father's vision; very well, life seemed to be saying, here is something that will certainly pass for an apocalypse until the real thing comes along. I had inclined to be contemptuous of my father for the conditions of his life, for the conditions of our lives. When his life had ended I began to wonder about that life and also, in a new way, to be apprehensive about my own.

I had not known my father very well. We had got on badly, partly because we shared, in our different fashions, the vice of stubborn pride. When he was dead I realized that I had hardly ever spoken to him. When he had been dead a long time I began to wish I had. It seems to be typical of life in America, where opportunities, real and fancied, are thicker than anywhere else on the globe, that the second generation has no time to talk to the first. No one, including my father, seems to have known exactly how old he was, but his mother had been born during slavery. He was of the first generation of free men. He, along with thousands of other Negroes, came North after 1919 and I was part of that generation which had never seen the landscape of what Negroes sometimes call the Old Country.

He had been born in New Orleans and had been a quite young man there during the time that Louis Armstrong, a boy, was running errands for the dives and honky-tonks of what was always presented to me as one of the most wicked of cities—to this day, whenever I think of New Orleans, I also helplessly think of Sodom and Gomorrah. My father never mentioned Louis Armstrong, except to forbid us to play his records; but there was a picture of him on our wall for a long time. One of my father's strong-willed female relatives had placed it there and forbade my father to take it down. He never did, but he eventually maneuvered her out of the house and when, some years later, she was in trouble and near death, he refused to do anything to help her.

He was, I think, very handsome. I gather this from photographs and from my own memories of him, dressed in his Sunday best and on his way to preach a sermon somewhere, when I was little. Handsome, proud, and ingrown, "like a toe-nail," somebody said. But he looked to me, as I grew older, like pictures I had seen of African tribal chieftains: he really should have been naked, with war-paint on and barbaric mementos, standing among spears. He could be chilling in the pulpit and indescribably cruel in his personal life and he was certainly the most bitter man I have ever met; yet it must be said that there was something else in him, buried in him, which lent him his tremendous power and, even, a rather crushing charm. It had something to do with his blackness, I think—he was very black—with his blackness and his beauty, and with the fact that he knew that he was black but did not know that he was beautiful. He claimed to be proud of his blackness but it had also been the cause of much humiliation and it had fixed bleak boundaries to his life. He was not a young man when we were growing up and he had already suffered many kinds of ruin; in his outrageously demanding and protective way he loved his children, who were black like him and menaced, like him; and all these things sometimes showed in his face when he tried, never to my knowledge with any success, to establish contact with any of us. When he took one of his children on his knee to play, the child always became fretful and began to cry; when he tried to help one of us with our homework the absolutely unabating tension which emanated from him caused our minds and our tongues to become paralyzed, so that he, scarcely knowing why, flew into a rage and the child, not knowing why, was punished. If it ever entered his head to bring a surprise home for his children, it was, almost unfailingly, the wrong surprise and even the big watermelons he often brought home on his back in the summertime led to the most appalling scenes. I do not remember, in all those years, that one of his children was ever glad to see him come home. From what I was able to gather of his early life, it seemed that this inability to establish contact with other people had always marked him and had been one of the things which had driven him out of New Orleans. There was something in him, therefore, groping and tentative, which was never expressed and which was buried with him. One saw it most clearly when he was facing new people and hoping to impress them. But he never did, not for long. We went from church to smaller and more improbable church, he found himself in less and less demand as a minister, and by the time he died none of his friends had come to see him for a long time. He had lived and died in an intolerable bitterness of spirit and it frightened me, as we drove him to the graveyard through

those unquiet, ruined streets, to see how powerful
and overflowing this bitterness could be and to
realize that this bitterness now was mine.

When he died I had been away from home for
a little over a year. In that year I had had time to
become aware of the meaning of all my father's
bitter warnings, had discovered the secret of his
proudly pursed lips and rigid carriage: I had discovered the weight of white people in the world.
I saw that this had been for my ancestors and now
would be for me an awful thing to live with and
that the bitterness which had helped to kill my
father could also kill me.

He had been ill a long time——in the mind, as
we now realized, reliving instances of his fantastic
intransigence in the new light of his affliction and
endeavoring to feel a sorrow for him which never,
quite, came true. We had not known that he was
being eaten up by paranoia, and the discovery that

his cruelty, to our bodies and our minds, had been one of the symptoms of his illness was not, then, enough to enable us to forgive him. The younger children felt, quite simply, relief that he would not be coming home anymore. My mother's observation that it was he, after all, who had kept them alive all these years meant nothing because the problems of keeping children alive are not real for children. The older children felt, with my father gone, that they could invite their friends to the house without fear that their friends would be insulted or, as had sometimes happened with me, being told that their friends were in league with the devil and intended to rob our family of everything we owned. (I didn't fail to wonder, and it made me hate him, what on earth we owned that anybody else would want.)

His illness was beyond all hope of healing before anyone realized that he was ill. He had always been so strange and had lived, like a prophet, in such unimaginably close communion with the Lord that his long silences which were punctuated by moans and hallelujahs and snatches of old songs while he sat at the living-room window never seemed odd to us. It was not until he refused to eat because, he said, his family was trying to poison him that my mother was forced to accept as a fact what had, until then, been only an unwilling suspicion. When he was committed, it was discovered that he had tuberculosis and, as it turned out, the disease of his mind allowed the disease of his body to destroy him. For the doctors could not force him to eat, either, and, though he was fed intravenously, it was clear from the beginning that there was no hope for him.

In my mind's eye I could see him, sitting at the window, locked up in his terrors; hating and fearing every living soul including his children who had betrayed him, too, by reaching towards the world which had despised him. There were nine of us. I began to wonder what it could have felt like for such a man to have had nine children whom he could barely feed. He used to make little jokes about our poverty, which never, of course, seemed very funny to us; they could not have seemed very funny to him, either, or else our all too feeble response to them would never have caused such rages. He spent great energy and achieved, to our chagrin, no small amount of success in keeping us away from the people who surrounded us, people who had all-night rent parties to which we listened when we should have been sleeping, people who cursed and drank and flashed razor blades on Lenox Avenue. He could not understand why, if they had so much energy to spare, they could not use it to make their lives better. He treated almost everybody on our block with a most uncharitable asperity and neither they, nor, of course, their children were slow to reciprocate.

The only white people who came to our house were welfare workers and bill collectors. It was almost always my mother who dealt with them, for my father's temper, which was at the mercy of his pride, was never to be trusted. It was clear that he felt their very presence in his home to be a violation: this was conveyed by his carriage, almost ludicrously stiff, and by his voice, harsh and vindictively polite. When I was around nine or ten I wrote a play which was directed by a young, white schoolteacher, a woman, who then took an interest in me, and gave me books to read and, in order to corroborate my theatrical bent, decided to take me to see what she somewhat tactlessly referred to as "real" plays. Theater-going was forbidden in our house, but, with the really cruel intuitiveness of a child, I suspected that the color

of this woman's skin would carry the day for me.
When, at school, she suggested taking me to the
theater, I did not, as I might have done if she had
been a Negro, find a way of discouraging her, but
agreed that she should pick me up at my house
one evening. I then, very cleverly, left all the rest
to my mother, who suggested to my father, as I
knew she would, that it would not be very nice to
let such a kind woman make the trip for nothing.
Also, since it was a schoolteacher, I imagine that
my mother countered the idea of sin with the idea
of "education," which word, even with my father,
carried a kind of bitter weight.

Before the teacher came my father took me
aside to ask *why* she was coming, what *interest* she
could possibly have in our house, in a boy like me.
I said I didn't know but I, too, suggested that it
had something to do with education. And I understood that my father was waiting for me to say

something——I didn't quite know what; perhaps
that I wanted his protection against this teacher
and her "education." I said none of these things and
the teacher came and we went out. It was clear,
during the brief interview in our living room, that
my father was agreeing very much against his will
and that he would have refused permission if he
had dared. The fact that he did not dare caused me
to despise him: I had no way of knowing that he
was facing in that living room a wholly unprecedented and frightening situation.

Later, when my father had been laid off from
his job, this woman became very important to us.
She was really a very sweet and generous woman
and went to a great deal of trouble to be of help
to us, particularly during one awful winter. My
mother called her by the highest name she knew:
she said she was a "christian." My father could
scarcely disagree but during the four or five years

of our relatively close association he never trusted her and was always trying to surprise in her open, Midwestern face the genuine, cunningly hidden, and hideous motivation. In later years, particularly when it began to be clear that this "education" of mine was going to lead me to perdition, he became more explicit and warned me that my white friends in high school were not really my friends and that I would see, when I was older, how white people would do anything to keep a Negro down. Some of them could be nice, he admitted, but none of them were to be trusted and most of them were not even nice. The best thing was to have as little to do with them as possible. I did not feel this way and I was certain, in my innocence, that I never would.

But the year which preceded my father's death had made a great change in my life. I had been living in New Jersey, working in defense plants, working and living among southerners, white and black. I knew about the south, of course, and about how southerners treated Negroes and how they expected them to behave, but it had never entered my mind that anyone would look at me and expect *me* to behave that way. I learned in New Jersey that to be a Negro meant, precisely, that one was never looked at but was simply at the mercy of the reflexes the color of one's skin caused in other people. I acted in New Jersey as I had always acted, that is as though I thought a great deal of myself—I had to *act* that way—with results that were, simply, unbelievable. I had scarcely arrived before I had earned the enmity, which was extraordinarily ingenious, of all my superiors and nearly all my co-workers. In the beginning, to make matters worse, I simply did not know what was happening. I did not know what I had done, and I shortly began to wonder what *anyone* could possibly do,

to bring about such unanimous, active, and un-
bearably vocal hostility. I knew about jim-crow
but I had never experienced it. I went to the same
self-service restaurant three times and stood with
all the Princeton boys before the counter, waiting
for a hamburger and coffee; it was always an extraordinarily long time before anything was set
before me; but it was not until the fourth visit
that I learned that, in fact, nothing had ever been
set before me: I had simply picked something up.
Negroes were not served there, I was told, and
they had been waiting for me to realize that I was
always the only Negro present. Once I was told
this, I determined to go there all the time. But
now they were ready for me and, though some
dreadful scenes were subsequently enacted in that
restaurant, I never ate there again.

It was the same story all over New Jersey, in
bars, bowling alleys, diners, places to live. I was

always being forced to leave, silently, or with mutual imprecations. I very shortly became notorious and children giggled behind me when I passed and their elders whispered or shouted—they really believed that I was mad. And it did begin to work on my mind, of course; I began to be afraid to go anywhere and to compensate for this I went places to which I really should not have gone and where, God knows, I had no desire to be. My reputation in town naturally enhanced my reputation at work and my working day became one long series of acrobatics designed to keep me out of trouble. I cannot say that these acrobatics succeeded. It began to seem that the machinery of the organization I worked for was turning over, day and night, with but one aim: to eject me. I was fired once, and contrived, with the aid of a friend from New York, to get back on the payroll; was fired again, and bounced back again. It took a while to fire me for the third time, but the third time took. There were no loopholes anywhere. There was not even any way of getting back inside the gates.

That year in New Jersey lives in my mind as though it were the year during which, having an unsuspected predilection for it, I first contracted some dread, chronic disease, the unfailing symptom of which is a kind of blind fever, a pounding in the skull and fire in the bowels. Once this disease is contracted, one can never be really carefree again, for the fever, without an instant's warning, can recur at any moment. It can wreck more important things than race relations. There is not a Negro alive who does not have this rage in his blood—one has the choice, merely, of living with it consciously or surrendering to it. As for me, this fever has recurred in me, and does, and will until the day I die.

My last night in New Jersey, a white friend from New York took me to the nearest big town,

Trenton, to go to the movies and have a few drinks. As it turned out, he also saved me from, at the very least, a violent whipping. Almost every detail of that night stands out very clearly in my memory. I even remember the name of the movie we saw because its title impressed me as being so patly ironical. It was a movie about the German occupation of France, starring Maureen O'Hara and Charles Laughton and called *This Land Is Mine*. I remember the name of the diner we walked into when the movie ended: it was the "American Diner." When we walked in the counterman asked what we wanted and I remember answering with the casual sharpness which had become my habit: "We want a hamburger and a cup of coffee, what do you think we want?" I do not know why, after a year of such rebuffs, I so completely failed to anticipate his answer, which was, of course, "We don't serve Negroes here." This reply failed to discompose me, at least for the moment. I made some sardonic comment about the name of the diner and we walked out into the streets.

This was the time of what was called the "brown-out," when the lights in all American cities were very dim. When we re-entered the streets something happened to me which had the force of an optical illusion, or a nightmare. The streets were very crowded and I was facing north. People were moving in every direction but it seemed to me, in that instant, that all of the people I could see, and many more than that, were moving toward me, against me, and that everyone was white. I remember how their faces gleamed. And I felt, like a physical sensation, a *click* at the nape of my neck as though some interior string connecting my head to my body had been cut. I began to walk. I heard my friend call after me, but I ignored him. Heaven only knows what was going on in his mind, but he had the good sense not to touch me—I don't know what would have happened if he had—and to keep me in sight. I don't know what was going on in my mind, either; I certainly had no conscious plan. I wanted to do something to crush these white faces, which were crushing me. I walked for perhaps a block or two until I came to an enormous, glittering, and fashionable restaurant in which I knew not even the intercession of the Virgin would cause me to be served. I pushed through the doors and took the first vacant seat I saw, at a table for two, and waited.

I do not know how long I waited and I rather wonder, until today, what I could possibly have looked like. Whatever I looked like, I frightened the waitress who shortly appeared, and the moment she appeared all of my fury flowed towards her. I hated her for her white face, and for her great, astounded, frightened eyes. I felt that if she found a black man so frightening I would make her fright worth-while.

She did not ask me what I wanted, but repeated, as though she had learned it somewhere, "We don't serve Negroes here." She did not say it with the blunt, derisive hostility to which I had grown so accustomed, but, rather, with a note of apology in her voice, and fear. This made me colder and more murderous than ever. I felt I had to do something with my hands. I wanted her to come close enough for me to get her neck between my hands.

So I pretended not to have understood her, hoping to draw her closer. And she did step a very short step closer, with her pencil poised incongruously over her pad, and repeated the formula: ". . . don't serve Negroes here."

Somehow, with the repetition of that phrase, which was already ringing in my head like a thousand bells of a nightmare, I realized that she would never come any closer and that I would have to strike from a distance. There was nothing on the table but an ordinary water-mug half full of water, and I picked this up and hurled it with all my strength at her. She ducked and it missed her and shattered against the mirror behind the bar. And, with that sound, my frozen blood abruptly thawed, I returned from wherever I had been, I *saw*, for the first time, the restaurant, the people with their mouths open, already, as it seemed to me, rising as one man, and I realized what I had done, and where I was, and I was frightened. I rose and began running for the door. A round, potbellied man grabbed me by the nape of the neck just as I reached the doors and began to beat me about the face. I kicked him and got loose and ran into the streets. My friend whispered, "*Run!*" and I ran.

My friend stayed outside the restaurant long enough to misdirect my pursuers and the police, who arrived, he told me, at once. I do not know what I said to him when he came to my room that night. I could not have said much. I felt, in the oddest, most awful way, that I had somehow betrayed him. I lived it over and over and over again, the way one relives an automobile accident after it has happened and one finds oneself alone and safe. I could not get over two facts, both equally difficult for the imagination to grasp, and one was that I could have been murdered. But the other was that I had been ready to commit murder. I saw nothing very clearly but I did see this: that my life, my *real* life, was in danger, and not from anything other people might do but from the hatred I carried in my own heart.

II

I had returned home around the second week in June—in great haste because it seemed that my father's death and my mother's confinement were both but a matter of hours. In the case of my mother, it soon became clear that she had simply made a miscalculation. This had always been her tendency and I don't believe that a single one of us arrived in the world, or has since arrived anywhere else, on time. But none of us dawdled so intolerably about the business of being born as did my baby sister. We sometimes amused ourselves, during those endless, stifling weeks, by picturing the baby sitting within in the safe, warm dark, bitterly regretting the necessity of becoming a part of our chaos and stubbornly putting it off as long as possible. I understood her perfectly and congratulated her on showing such good sense so soon. Death, however, sat as purposefully at my father's bedside as life stirred within my mother's womb and it was harder to understand why he so lingered in that long shadow. It seemed that he had bent, and for a long time, too, all of his energies towards dying. Now death was ready for him but my father held back.

All of Harlem, indeed, seemed to be infected by waiting. I had never before known it to be so violently still. Racial tensions throughout this country were exacerbated during the early years of the war, partly because the labor market brought together hundreds of thousands of ill-prepared people and partly because Negro soldiers, regardless of where they were born, received their military training in the south. What happened in defense plants and army camps had repercussions, naturally, in every Negro ghetto. The situation in Harlem had grown bad enough for clergymen, policemen, educators, politicians, and social workers to assert in one breath that there was no "crime wave" and to offer, in the very next breath, suggestions as to how to combat it. These suggestions always seemed to involve playgrounds, despite the fact that racial skirmishes were occurring in the playgrounds, too. Playground or not, crime wave or not, the Harlem police force had been augmented in March, and the unrest grew—perhaps, in fact, partly as a result of the ghetto's instinctive hatred of policemen. Perhaps the most revealing news item, out of the steady parade of reports of muggings, stabbings, shootings, assaults, gang wars, and accusations of police brutality, is the item concerning six Negro girls who set upon a white girl in the subway because, as they all too accurately put it, she was stepping on their toes. Indeed she was, all over the nation.

I had never before been so aware of policemen, on foot, on horseback, on corners, everywhere, always two by two. Nor had I ever been so aware of small knots of people. They were on stoops and on corners and in doorways, and what was striking about them, I think, was that they did not seem to be talking. Never, when I passed these groups, did the usual sound of a curse or a laugh ring out and neither did there seem to be any hum of gossip. There was certainly, on the other hand, occurring between them communication extraordinarily intense. Another thing that was striking was the unexpected diversity of the people who made up these groups. Usually, for example, one would see a group of sharpies standing on the street corner, jiving the passing chicks; or a group of older men, usually, for some reason, in the vicinity of a barber shop, discussing baseball

scores, or the numbers, or making rather chilling observations about women they had known.
Women, in a general way, tended to be seen less
often together—unless they were church women,
or very young girls, or prostitutes met together
for an unprofessional instant. But that summer I
saw the strangest combinations: large, respectable,
churchly matrons standing on the stoops or the
corners with their hair tied up, together with a girl
in sleazy satin whose face bore the marks of gin and
the razor, or heavy-set, abrupt, no-nonsense older
men, in company with the most disreputable and
fanatical "race" men, or these same "race" men with
the sharpies, or these sharpies with the churchly
women. Seventh Day Adventists and Methodists
and Spiritualists seemed to be hobnobbing with
Holyrollers and they were all, alike, entangled
with the most flagrant disbelievers; something
heavy in their stance seemed to indicate that they

had all, incredibly, seen a common vision, and on each face there seemed to be the same strange, bitter shadow.

The churchly women and the matter-of-fact, no-nonsense men had children in the Army. The sleazy girls they talked to had lovers there, the sharpies and the "race" men had friends and brothers there. It would have demanded an unquestioning patriotism, happily as uncommon in this country as it is undesirable, for these people not to have been disturbed by the bitter letters they received, by the newspaper stories they read, not to have been enraged by the posters, then to be found all over New York, which described the Japanese as "yellow-bellied Japs." It was only the "race" men, to be sure, who spoke ceaselessly of being revenged—how this vengeance was to be exacted was not clear—for the indignities and dangers suffered by Negro boys in uniform; but everybody felt a directionless, hopeless bitterness, as well as that panic which can scarcely be suppressed when one knows that a human being one loves is beyond one's reach, and in danger. This helplessness and this gnawing uneasiness does something, at length, to even the toughest mind. Perhaps the best way to sum all this up is to say that the people I knew felt, mainly, a peculiar kind of relief when they knew that their boys were being shipped out of the south, to do battle overseas. It was, perhaps, like feeling that the most dangerous part of a dangerous journey had been passed and that now, even if death should come, it would come with honor and without the complicity of their countrymen. Such a death would be, in short, a fact with which one could hope to live.

It was on the 28th of July, which I believe was a Wednesday, that I visited my father for the first time during his illness and for the last time in his life. The moment I saw him I knew why I had put off this visit so long. I had told my mother that I did not want to see him because I hated him. But this was not true. It was only that I *had* hated him and I wanted to hold on to this hatred. I did not want to look on him as a ruin: it was not a ruin I had hated. I imagine that one of the reasons people cling to their hates so stubbornly is because they sense, once hate is gone, that they will be forced to deal with pain.

We traveled out to him, his older sister and myself, to what seemed to be the very end of a very Long Island. It was hot and dusty and we wrangled, my aunt and I, all the way out, over the fact that I had recently begun to smoke and, as she said, to give myself airs. But I knew that she wrangled with me because she could not bear to face the fact of her brother's dying. Neither could I endure the reality of her despair, her unstated bafflement as to what had happened to her brother's life, and her own. So we wrangled and I smoked and from time to time she fell into a heavy reverie. Covertly, I watched her face, which was the face of an old woman; it had fallen in, the eyes were sunken and lightless; soon she would be dying, too.

In my childhood—it had not been so long ago—I had thought her beautiful. She had been quick-witted and quick-moving and very generous with all the children and each of her visits had been an event. At one time one of my brothers and myself had thought of running away to live with her. Now she could no longer produce out of her handbag some unexpected and yet familiar delight. She made me feel pity and revulsion and fear. It was awful to realize that she no longer caused me to feel affection. The closer we came to the hospital the more querulous she became and at the same time, naturally, grew more dependent on me. Between pity and guilt and fear I began to feel that there was another me trapped in my skull like a jack-in-the-box who might escape my control at any moment and fill the air with screaming.

She began to cry the moment we entered the room and she saw him lying there, all shriveled and still, like a little black monkey. The great, gleaming apparatus which fed him and would have compelled him to be still even if he had been able to move brought to mind, not beneficence, but torture; the tubes entering his arm made me think of pictures I had seen when a child, of Gulliver, tied down by the pygmies on that island. My aunt wept and wept, there was a whistling sound in my father's throat; nothing was said; he could not speak. I wanted to take his hand, to say something. But I do not know what I could have said, even if he could have heard me. He was not really in that room with us, he had at last really embarked on his journey; and though my aunt told me that he said he was going to meet Jesus, I did not hear anything except that whistling in his throat. The doctor came back and we left, into that unbearable train again, and home. In the morning came the telegram saying that he was dead. Then the house was suddenly full of relatives, friends, hysteria, and confusion and I quickly left my mother and the children to the care of those impressive women, who, in Negro communities at least, automatically appear at times of bereavement armed with lotions, proverbs, and patience, and an ability to cook. I went downtown. By the time I returned, later the same day, my mother had been carried to the hospital and the baby had been born.

III

For my father's funeral I had nothing black to wear
and this posed a nagging problem all day long. It
was one of those problems, simple, or impossible
of solution, to which the mind insanely clings in
order to avoid the mind's real trouble. I spent most
of that day at the downtown apartment of a girl I
knew, celebrating my birthday with whiskey and
wondering what to wear that night. When plan-
ning a birthday celebration one naturally does not
expect that it will be up against competition from
a funeral and this girl had anticipated taking me
out that night, for a big dinner and a night club
afterwards. Sometime during the course of that
long day we decided that we would go out anyway, when my father's funeral service was over.
I imagine *I* decided it, since, as the funeral hour
approached, it became clearer and clearer to me

that I would not know what to do with myself when it was over. The girl, stifling her very lively concern as to the possible effects of the whiskey on one of my father's chief mourners, concentrated on being conciliatory and practically helpful. She found a black shirt for me somewhere and ironed it and, dressed in the darkest pants and jacket I owned, and slightly drunk, I made my way to my father's funeral.

The chapel was full, but not packed, and very quiet. There were, mainly, my father's relatives, and his children, and here and there I saw faces I had not seen since childhood, the faces of my father's one-time friends. They were very dark and solemn now, seeming somehow to suggest that they had known all along that something like this would happen. Chief among the mourners was my aunt, who had quarreled with my father all his life; by which I do not mean to suggest that her mourning was insincere or that she had not loved him. I suppose that she was one of the few people in the world who had, and their incessant quarreling proved precisely the strength of the tie that bound them. The only other person in the world, as far as I knew, whose relationship to my father rivaled my aunt's in depth was my mother, who was not there.

It seemed to me, of course, that it was a very long funeral. But it was, if anything, a rather shorter funeral than most, nor, since there were no overwhelming, uncontrollable expressions of grief, could it be called—if I dare to use the word—successful. The minister who preached my father's funeral sermon was one of the few my father had still been seeing as he neared his end. He presented to us in his sermon a man whom none of us had ever seen—a man thoughtful, patient, and forbearing, a Christian inspiration to all who knew him, and a model for his children. And no doubt the children, in their disturbed and guilty state, were almost ready to believe this; he had been remote enough to be anything and, anyway, the shock of the incontrovertible, that it was really our father lying up there in that casket, prepared the mind for anything. His sister moaned and this grief-stricken moaning was taken as corroboration. The other faces held a dark, non-committal thoughtfulness. This was not the man they had known, but they had scarcely expected to be confronted with *him*; this was, in a sense deeper than questions of fact, the man they had not known, and the man they had not known may have been the real one. The real man, whoever he had been, had suffered and now he was dead: this was all that was sure and all that mattered now. Every man in the chapel hoped that when his hour came he, too, would be eulogized, which is to say forgiven, and that all of his lapses, greeds, errors, and strayings from the truth would be invested with coherence and looked upon with charity. This was perhaps the last thing human beings could give each other and it was what they demanded, after all, of the Lord. Only the Lord saw the midnight tears, only He was present when one of His children, moaning and wringing hands, paced up and down the room. When one slapped one's child in anger the recoil in the heart reverberated through heaven and became part of the pain of the universe. And when the children were hungry and sullen and distrustful and one watched them, daily, growing wilder, and further away, and running headlong into danger, it was the Lord who knew what the charged heart endured as the strap was laid to the backside; the Lord alone who knew what one *would* have said if one had had, like the Lord, the gift of the living word. It was the Lord who knew of the impossibility every parent in that room faced: how to prepare the child for the day when the child would be despised and how to *create* in the child—by what means?—a stronger antidote to this poison than one had found for oneself. The avenues, side streets, bars, billiard halls, hospitals, police stations, and even the playgrounds of Harlem—not to mention the houses of correction, the jails, and the morgue—testified to the potency of the poison while remaining silent as to the efficacy of whatever antidote, irresistibly raising the question of whether or not such an antidote existed; raising, which was worse, the question of whether or not an antidote was desirable; perhaps poison should be fought with poison. With these several schisms in the mind and with more terrors in the heart than could be named, it was better not to judge the man who had gone down under an impossible burden. It was better to remember:

*Thou knowest this man's fall; but thou knowest not his
wrassling.*

While the preacher talked and I watched the
children—years of changing their diapers, scrub-
bing them, slapping them, taking them to school,
and scolding them had had the perhaps inevitable
result of making me love them, though I am not
sure I knew this then—my mind was busily break-
ing out with a rash of disconnected impressions.
Snatches of popular songs, indecent jokes, bits of
books I had read, movie sequences, faces, voices,
political issues—I thought I was going mad; all
these impressions suspended, as it were, in the
solution of the faint nausea produced in me by the
heat and liquor. For a moment I had the impression
that my alcoholic breath, inefficiently disguised
with chewing gum, filled the entire chapel. Then
someone began singing one of my father's favorite
songs and, abruptly, I was with him, sitting on

his knee, in the hot, enormous, crowded church which was the first church we attended. It was the Abyssinia Baptist Church on 138th Street. We had not gone there long. With this image, a host of others came. I had forgotten, in the rage of my growing up, how proud my father had been of me when I was little. Apparently, I had had a voice and my father had liked to show me off before the members of the church. I had forgotten what he had looked like when he was pleased but now I remembered that he had always been grinning with pleasure when my solos ended. I even remembered certain expressions on his face when he teased my mother——had he loved her? I would never know. And when had it all begun to change? For now it seemed that he had not always been cruel. I remembered being taken for a haircut and scraping my knee on the footrest of the barber's chair and I remembered my father's face as he soothed my crying and applied the stinging iodine. Then I remembered our fights, fights which had been of the worst possible kind because my technique had been silence.

I remembered the one time in all our life together when we had really spoken to each other.

It was on a Sunday and it must have been shortly before I left home. We were walking, just the two of us, in our usual silence, to or from church. I was in high school and had been doing a lot of writing and I was, at about this time, the editor of the high school magazine. But I had also been a Young Minister and had been preaching from the pulpit. Lately, I had been taking fewer engagements and preached as rarely as possible. It was said in the church, quite truthfully, that I was "cooling off."

My father asked me abruptly, "You'd rather write than preach, wouldn't you?"

I was astonished at his question—because it was a real question. I answered, "Yes."

That was all we said. It was awful to remember that that was all we had *ever* said.

The casket now was opened and the mourners were being led up the aisle to look for the last time on the deceased. The assumption was that the family was too overcome with grief to be allowed to make this journey alone and I watched while my aunt was led to the casket and, muffled in black, and shaking, led back to her seat. I disapproved of forcing the children to look on their dead father, considering that the shock of his death, or, more truthfully, the shock of death as a reality, was already a little more than a child could bear, but my judgment in this matter had been overruled and there they were, bewildered and frightened and very small, being led, one by one, to the casket. But there is also something very gallant about children at such moments. It has something to do with their silence and gravity and with the fact that one cannot help them. Their legs, somehow, seem *exposed*, so that it is at once incredible and terribly clear that their legs are all they have to hold them up.

I had not wanted to go to the casket myself and I certainly had not wished to be led there, but there was no way of avoiding either of these forms. One of the deacons led me up and I looked on my father's face. I cannot say that it looked like him at all. His blackness had been equivocated by powder and there was no suggestion in that casket of what his power had or could have been. He was simply an old man dead, and it was hard to believe that he had ever given anyone either joy or pain. Yet, his life filled that room. Further up the avenue his wife was holding his newborn child. Life and death so close together, and love and hatred, and right and wrong, said something to me which I did not want to hear concerning man, concerning the life of man.

After the funeral, while I was downtown desperately celebrating my birthday, a Negro soldier, in the lobby of the Hotel Braddock, got into a fight with a white policeman over a Negro girl. Negro girls, white policemen, in or out of uniform, and Negro males—in or out of uniform—were part of the furniture of the lobby of the Hotel Braddock and this was certainly not the first time such an incident had occurred. It was destined, however, to receive an unprecedented publicity, for the fight between the policeman and the soldier ended with the shooting of the soldier. Rumor, flowing immediately to the streets outside, stated that the soldier had been shot in the back, an instantaneous and revealing invention, and that the soldier had died protecting a Negro woman. The facts were somewhat different—for example, the soldier had not been shot in the back, and was not dead, and the girl seems to have been as dubious a symbol of womanhood as her white counterpart in Georgia usually is, but no one was interested in the facts. They preferred the invention because this invention expressed and corroborated their hates and fears so perfectly. It is just as well to remember that people are always doing this. Perhaps many of those legends, including Christianity, to which the world clings began their conquest of the world with just some such concerted surrender to distortion. The effect, in Harlem, of this particular legend was like the effect of a lit match in a tin of gasoline. The mob gathered before the doors of the Hotel Braddock simply began to swell and to spread in every direction, and Harlem exploded.

The mob did not cross the ghetto lines. It would have been easy, for example, to have gone over Morningside Park on the west side or to have crossed the Grand Central railroad tracks at 125th Street on the east side, to wreak havoc in white neighborhoods. The mob seems to have been mainly interested in something more potent and real than the white face, that is, in white power, and the principal damage done during the riot of the summer of 1943 was to white business establishments in Harlem. It might have been a far bloodier story, of course, if, at the hour the riot began, these establishments had still been open. From the Hotel Braddock the mob fanned out, east and west along 125th Street, and for the entire length of Lenox, Seventh, and Eighth avenues. Along each of these avenues, and along each major side street—116th, 125th, 135th, and so on—bars, stores, pawnshops, restaurants, even little luncheonettes had been smashed open and entered and looted—looted, it might be added, with more haste than efficiency. The shelves really looked as though a bomb had struck them. Cans of beans and soup and dog food, along with toilet paper, corn flakes, sardines and milk tumbled every which way, and abandoned cash registers and cases of beer leaned crazily out of the splintered windows and were strewn along the avenues. Sheets, blankets, and clothing of every description formed a kind of path, as though people had dropped them while running. I truly had not realized that Harlem *had* so many stores until I saw them all smashed open; the first time the word *wealth* ever entered my mind in relation to Harlem was when I saw it scattered in the streets. But one's first, incongruous impression of plenty was countered immediately by an impression of waste. None of this was doing anybody any good. It would have been better to have left the plate glass as it had been and the goods lying in the stores.

It would have been better, but it would also have been intolerable, for Harlem had needed something to smash. To smash something is the ghetto's chronic need. Most of the time it is the members of the ghetto who smash each other, and themselves. But as long as the ghetto walls are standing there will always come a moment when these outlets do not work. That summer, for example, it was not enough to get into a fight on Lenox Avenue, or curse out one's cronies in the barber shops. If ever, indeed, the violence which fills Harlem's churches, pool halls, and bars erupts outward in a more direct fashion, Harlem and its citizens are likely to vanish in an apocalyptic flood. That this is not likely to happen is due to a great many reasons, most hidden and powerful among them the Negro's real relation to the white American. This relation prohibits, simply, anything as uncomplicated and satisfactory as pure hatred.

In order really to hate white people, one has to blot so much out of the mind—and the heart—that this hatred itself becomes an exhausting and self-destructive pose. But this does not mean, on the other hand, that love comes easily: the white world is too powerful, too complacent, too ready with gratuitous humiliation, and, above all, too ignorant and too innocent for that. One is absolutely forced to make perpetual qualifications and one's own reactions are always canceling each other out. It is this, really, which has driven so many people mad, both white and black. One is always in the position of having to decide between amputation and gangrene. Amputation is swift but time may prove that the amputation was not necessary—or one may delay the amputation too long. Gangrene is slow, but it is impossible to be sure that one is reading one's symptoms right. The idea of going through life as a cripple is more than one can bear, and equally unbearable is the risk of swelling up slowly, in agony, with poison. And the trouble, finally, is that the risks are real even if the choices do not exist.

"But as for me and my house," my father had said, "we will serve the Lord." I wondered, as we drove him to his resting place, what this line had meant for him. I had heard him preach it many times. I had preached it once myself, proudly giving it an interpretation different from my father's. Now the whole thing came back to me, as though my father and I were on our way to Sunday school and I were memorizing the golden text: *And if it seem evil unto you to serve the Lord, choose you this day whom you will serve; whether the gods which your fathers served that were on the other side of the flood, or the gods of the Amorites, in whose land ye dwell: but as for me and my house, we will serve the Lord.* I suspected in these familiar lines a meaning which had never been there for me before. All of my father's texts and songs, which I had decided were meaningless, were arranged before me at his death like empty bottles, waiting to hold the meaning which life would give them for me. This was his legacy: nothing is ever escaped. That bleakly memorable morning I hated the unbelievable streets and the Negroes and whites who had, equally, made them that way. But I knew that it was folly, as my father would have said, this bitterness was folly. It was necessary to hold on to the things that mattered. The dead man mattered, the new life mattered; blackness and whiteness did not matter; to believe that they did was to acquiesce in one's own destruction. Hatred, which could destroy so much, never failed to destroy the man who hated and this was an immutable law.

It began to seem that one would have to hold in the mind forever two ideas which seemed to be in opposition. The first idea was acceptance, the acceptance, totally without rancor, of life as it is, and men as they are: in the light of this idea, it goes without saying that injustices is a commonplace. But this did not mean that one could be complacent, for the second idea was of equal power: that one must never, in one's own life, accept these injustices as commonplace but must fight them with all one's strength. This fight begins, however, in the heart and it now had been laid to my charge to keep my own heart free of hatred and despair. This intimation made my heart heavy and, now that my father was irrecoverable, I wished that he had been beside me so that I could have searched his face for the answers which only the future would give me now.

ABOUT
THE AUTHOR

JAMES BALDWIN (1924–1987) was a novelist, an essayist, a playwright, a poet, and a social critic, and one of America's foremost writers. His writing explores palpable yet unspoken intricacies of racial, sexual, and class distinctions in Western societies, most notably in mid-twentieth-century America. A Harlem, New York, native, he lived periodically in exile in the south of France and in Turkey. He is the author of several novels and books of nonfiction, including *Notes of a Native Son*, *Go Tell It on the Mountain*, *Giovanni's Room*, *Another*

Country, *Tell Me How Long the Train's Been Gone*, *If Beale Street Could Talk*, *Just Above My Head*, *The Fire Next Time*, *No Name in the Street*, and *The Evidence of Things Not Seen*, and of the poetry collection *Jimmy's Blues*.